Computer Wings

Newsletter Publisher

Course Book

Syllabus Version 1.0

First Edition 2009

ISBN 9780 7517 5751 4

British Library Cataloguing-in-Publication Data
A catalogue record for this book is available from the British Library

A joint publication from:

Q-Validus Ltd.

NovaUCD   t: + 353 1 716 3742
Belfield Innovation Park   e: info@computerwings.com
University College Dublin   w: www.computerwings.com
Dublin 4   w: www.q-validus.com
Ireland

BPP Learning Media Ltd.

BPP House, Aldine Place   t: 0845 0751 100 (within the UK)
London W12 8AA   t: +44 (0) 20 8740 2211
United Kingdom   e: learningmedia@bpp.com
                                 w: www.bpp.com/learningmedia

Computer Wings® is a registered trademark of Q-Validus Limited in Ireland and other countries. This Computer Wings approved training material may be used in assisting candidates to prepare for their Computer Wings certification test.

Candidates wishing to sit Computer Wings certification tests are required to pre-register for the programme. Candidates may register at any Authorised Centre.

Without registration no certification tests can be taken and no Computer Wings certificate or any other form of recognition may be awarded.

For any further information about Computer Wings visit www.computerwings.com

CONTENTS

What is Computer Wings?

Computer Wings is an exciting new practical computer skills certification programme for real world tasks and roles in the modern workplace.

The certification delivers knowledge and skills in a range of areas. The Computer Wings programme assists candidates to achieve increased efficiency, higher standards of output, greater levels of collaboration, and improved user confidence.

The Computer Wings programme covers the key functions within an organisation such as planning, project management, communication, marketing, IT, online business and process flows.

The Computer Wings programme is a flexible scheme, that allows Candidates to choose the module or modules which are most appropriate to their current or future roles.

Computer Wings provides a total programme solution, including registration, automated testing and certification, and supporting training materials.

For any further information visit www.computerwings.com

Scottish Qualifications Authority (SQA) endorsement

The Computer Wings qualification is mapped to the UK National Occupational Standards (NOS) and is endorsed by the Scottish Qualifications Authority (SQA). The Computer Wings programme has been credit rated and levelled for the Scottish Credit Qualifications Framework (SCQF).

Newsletter Publisher has been officially designated as SCQF level 7 with 5 credit points. To see the SCQF level and credits for all other Computer Wings Modules check out
http://www.computerwings.com/endorsements

Get certified

You now have your Computer Wings Course Book, which is designed to bring your skills to the next level. The next step is to prove your competencies by taking the Computer Wings certification test. Computer Wings is endorsed by the Scottish Qualifications Authority (SQA) www.sqa.co.uk, a world renowned awarding body.

Register for your test

To gain your Computer Wings certification you need to register for your test with a Computer Wings Authorised Centre.

Computer Wings certification tests are only available through Authorised Centres. For further information visit www.computerwings.com

Computer Wings overview

Computer Wings is an exciting new computer skills training and certification programme. The programme consists of ten standalone modules which focus on the productivity skills required in today's rapidly changing economy.

The Computer Wings certification programme comprises the following modules:

Project Manager

Plan, resource, execute and manage mid-sized projects to deliver high quality, well defined, organised results on time and on budget.

Mail Manager

Communicate and collaborate more effectively by becoming proficient in the use of email software to manage organisational scheduling and communication.

Diagram Maker

Enhance effective business communication by using diagram tools and image editing applications to create diagrams, images and conceptual schemes.

Newsletter Publisher

Produce professional quality newsletters, brochures, eshots or leaflets to support marketing activity and organisational communications.

Presenter Pro

Enhance business communications by developing the skills to create and deliver attractive, persuasive, and audience focused presentations.

Web Creator

Create and maintain informative and user-friendly websites to support internal and external communications.

Web Optimiser

Develop Search Engine Optimisation (SEO) skills to support and improve traffic, create more impact, and generate higher sales.

Web Analyser

Use web analysis tools to measure the appeal of a website, view the origin of visits and referrals, and generate reports about website activity.

IT TroubleShooter

Develop the IT administration skills required to deal with hardware, software, memory and network issues in small IT network environments.

IT GateKeeper

Recognise important software, hardware and network security considerations in order to protect small IT network environments.

Computer Wings benefits

The Computer Wings certification programme enables Candidates to develop their skills and confidently address computing applications relevant to their needs.

The Computer Wings certification programme delivers:

- A recognised and valuable qualification.

- Practical skills, competencies, and knowledge.

- Awareness of good practice, efficient and productive use of applications.

- Confidence to produce effective and professional looking outputs.

- Improved returns on human and ICT investments.

- Validation of skills and knowledge as evidenced by certification.

- A match between Candidate skills and organisational needs.

- Enhanced collaborative skills within an organisation.

- Improved productivity through more efficient use of office applications.

- Improved communication across the organisation.

Content validation

Q-Validus works with Subject Matter Experts (SME's) and renowned international awarding bodies and international partners, to develop and deliver Computer Wings, which reflects a comprehensive and recognised skills and knowledge standard.

Computer Wings Course Books are developed by SME's across the range of specialist domains.

Ongoing content validity of Computer Wings Syllabus standards definition is maintained by the Syllabus Expert Group (SEG) using the Q-Validus online Content Validation Database (CVD), a bespoke software tool for standards validation. Expert feedback and comment from around the world, in respect of Computer Wings Syllabus measuring points, is collated and recorded in the Content Validation Database. The current Computer Wings Syllabus Version is Syllabus Version 1.0. The ongoing standards validation process for Computer Wings supports the continuing applicability and relevance of Computer Wings.

Experts wishing to provide technical comments and feedback in relation to Computer Wings Course Books, or seeking to participate as experts in relation to the Computer Wings Syllabus standards definition, should contact: technical@computerwings.com

Computer Wings Newsletter Publisher overview

Computer Wings is an internationally recognised computer and ICT skills standard. Computer Wings training and certification programmes help Candidates work more effectively by developing computer and ICT skills that deliver valuable productivity benefits.

Computer Wings Newsletter Publisher is a certification in the area of desktop publishing. The core product referenced in this Course Book version is Microsoft Publisher 2007.

The Computer Wings Newsletter Publisher certification validates Candidate skill and knowledge in using publishing software to produce professional looking and effective newsletters, brochures or email shots to promote news, events, products or updates to clients or stakeholders.

Newsletter Publisher is designed to provide practical competence with the major features and functions of Microsoft Publisher and enable Candidates to produce valuable communications and marketing collateral such as newsletters, brochures, flyers or eshots.

Candidates shall:

- Develop the skills to produce newsletters, brochures, leaflets and eshots.
- Copy, move template based layouts and schemes.
- Add different layout elements such as text boxes, pictures, images.
- Link or unlink text boxes, recognise the text overflow symbol.
- Add columns and rows and change gutter width.
- Insert tables and change cell background colours.
- Modify text style, change text leading.
- Import pictures in different formats.
- Select images, and group or ungroup.
- Proof and output files to print, to PDF, or online.
- Republish developed Publisher content as a website.
- Recognise organisation branding guidelines or specifications.

Newsletter Publisher syllabus

Category	Skill area	Ref.	Measuring point
4.1 START	4.1.1 Setup	4.1.1.1	Open a desktop publishing application.
		4.1.1.2	Open a desktop publishing file, template.
		4.1.1.3	Create a project or new document.
		4.1.1.4	Close a project or document file.
		4.1.1.5	Close the desktop publishing application.
	4.1.2 Layout	4.1.2.1	Add a layout template to a project.
		4.1.2.2	Copy, move a layout.
		4.1.2.3	Delete a layout.
	4.1.3 View	4.1.3.1	Switch between project layouts.
		4.1.3.2	Activate an open project.
		4.1.3.3	Go to a project page.
		4.1.3.4	View a layout or project in multiple windows.
		4.1.3.5	Arrange different layout, project views.
		4.1.3.6	Change the zoom levels in or out.
	4.1.4 Save	4.1.4.1	Save a newsletter project.
		4.1.4.2	Save a new version of a project file.
		4.1.4.2	Revert to a last saved project file version.
4.2 TEXT	4.2.1 Text box	4.2.1.1	Add a text box.
		4.2.1.2	Move a text box manually, with precision.
		4.2.1.3	Resize a text box manually, with precision.
	4.2.2 Insert	4.2.2.1	Insert text.
		4.2.2.2	Select, delete text.
		4.2.2.3	Drag and drop text.
		4.2.2.4	Add text along a defined text path.
		4.2.2.5	Recognise the text overflow symbol.
	4.2.3 Manipulate	4.2.3.1	Add a border to a text box.
		4.2.3.2	Position text in its text box.
		4.2.3.3	Flip a text box.
		4.2.3.4	Rotate a text box manually, with precision.
		4.2.3.5	Change the text box vertical alignment.
		4.2.3.6	Add columns in a text box.
		4.2.3.7	Change text box gutter width.
		4.2.3.8	Save text to a word processing file.

Category	Skill area	Ref.	Measuring point
	4.2.4 Text Flow	4.2.4.1	Import text.
		4.2.4.2	Wrap text around a picture, text box.
		4.2.4.3	Insert, delete pages.
		4.2.4.4	Rearrange pages.
		4.2.4.5	Drag, copy pages from another layout or project.
		4.2.4.6	Link, unlink text boxes.
		4.2.4.7	Delete text in a text box chain.
		4.2.4.8	Unlink text in a text box chain.
4.3 FORMAT	4.3.1 Text	4.3.1.1	Change the font size, colour of text.
		4.3.1.2	Change style of text in a text box.
		4.3.1.3	Resize type.
		4.3.1.4	Change text leading.
		4.3.1.5	Kern text.
	4.3.2 Paragraphs	4.3.2.1	Indent first line of a paragraph.
		4.3.2.2	Create a new paragraph.
		4.3.2.3	Change spacing between paragraphs.
		4.3.2.4	Apply a soft paragraph return.
		4.3.2.5	Copy formats in the same project.
		4.3.2.6	Create, or edit hyphenation, justification.
4.4 TABLES	4.4.1 Inserts	4.4.1.1	Add a table.
		4.4.1.2	Add, edit, and remove text in a table.
		4.4.1.3	Resize a column or row.
		4.4.1.4	Change the border colour, styles in a table.
		4.4.1.5	Change the background colour of a table, cells.
		4.4.1.6	Add, delete rows or columns.
		4.4.1.7	Make cells or columns of consistent size.
		4.4.1.8	Merge cells in a table.
4.5 PICTURES	4.5.1 Inserts	4.5.1.1	Add a picture box.
		4.5.1.2	Import a picture in different formats.
		4.5.1.3	Recognise picture formats and their characteristics.

Category	Skill area	Ref.	Measuring point
	4.5.2 Position	4.5.2.1	Resize a picture box manually, with precision.
		4.5.2.2	Delete a picture box, delete picture only.
		4.5.2.3	Copy a picture box.
		4.5.2.4	Move a picture box manually, with precision.
		4.5.2.5	Scale, centre a picture in a picture box.
		4.5.2.6	Crop a picture within its picture box.
		4.5.2.7	Rotate, skew a picture.
		4.5.2.8	Flip a picture.
	4.5.3 Selection	4.5.3.1	Select all items in page, project.
		4.5.3.2	Select, de-select multiple items.
		4.5.3.3	Copy, move items within a page, between projects.
		4.5.3.4	Group, ungroup items.
		4.5.3.5	Remove an item from a group.
		4.5.3.6	Promote, demote items.
	4.5.4 Colour	4.5.4.1	Change a background colour.
		4.5.4.2	Change colour in a picture.
		4.5.4.3	Change the colour of a text box border.
4.6 DELIVER	4.6.1 Output	4.6.1.1	Preview a newsletter project including spell checking and proof reading, and make changes where necessary.
		4.6.1.2	Choose basic print options, and print.
		4.6.1.3	Output files in PDF format.
		4.6.1.4	Publish a newsletter in a website.
		4.6.1.5	Publish a newsletter within an email.
	4.6.1 Laws & Guidelines	4.6.2.1	Be aware of data protection legislation or conventions in your country.
		4.6.2.2	Be aware of copyright laws and their impact for downloading content from the Internet, and in terms of image usage, and apportion due credit for use.
		4.6.2.3	Recognise the significance of disability / equality legislation in helping to provide all users with access to information.
		4.6.2.4	Recognise organisation layout guidelines or branding specifications.

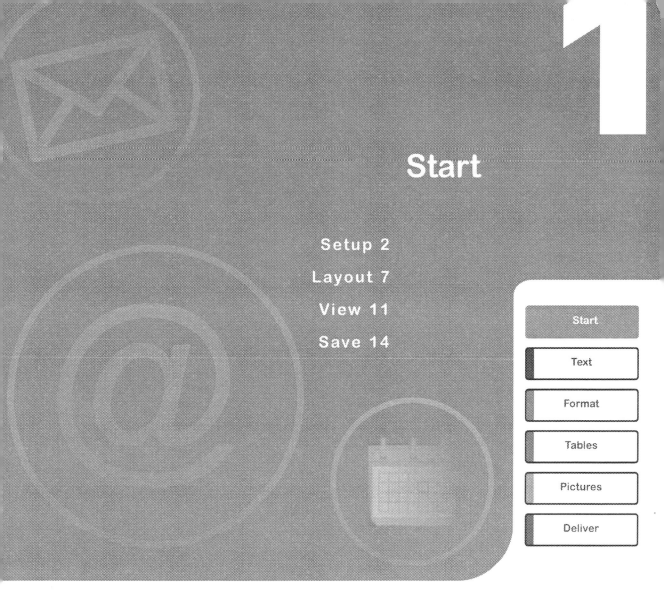

Start

Start

Text

Format

Tables

Pictures

Deliver

Measuring points

- ▶ Open a desktop publishing application
- ▶ Open a desktop publishing file, template
- ▶ Create a project or new document
- ▶ Close a project or document file
- ▶ Close the desktop publishing application
- ▶ Add a layout template to a project
- ▶ Copy, move a layout
- ▶ Delete a layout
- ▶ Switch between project layouts

- ▶ Activate an open project
- ▶ Go to a project page
- ▶ View a layout or project in multiple windows
- ▶ Arrange different layout, project views
- ▶ Change the zoom levels in or out
- ▶ Save a newsletter project
- ▶ Save a new version of a project file
- ▶ Revert to a last saved project file version

Introduction

Using Microsoft Publisher 2007, you can create professional communications material such as newsletters, brochures or leaflets to support marketing activity and organisational communications. You can use the numerous templates provided with Publisher as a basis for creating the layout and style for your publication.

This chapter describes the basics of accessing files and documents as well as some of the interface features that you need to know to use Publisher effectively.

Setup

This section describes how to start working with Publisher, how to create a new document and save it to your folder.

Opening Publisher

Publisher is available when you access your Microsoft Office applications. To open Publisher:

1. Open *Start* menu, select *All Programs*.

2. Select *Microsoft Office* from the available programs menu.

3. Select *Microsoft Office Publisher 2007*.

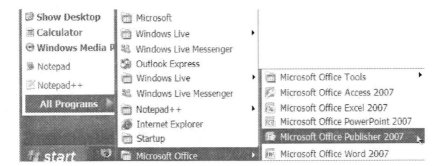

Publisher is opened and you can begin creating your own publications.

 There are many ways in which commands can be carried out with different software products; menus, toolbar icons, a keyboard command, or a right-click can all be used. A visual approach is taken as the main task pathway for learning here; for example, making text bold could be achieved by using a toolbar icon or the keyboard shortcut: *Ctrl+B*. Candidates and Trainers should be aware that in this Course Book a menu or dialogue based approach is used as the preferred learning pathway.

Working with Publisher

When you start Publisher, the *Getting Started with Microsoft Office Publisher 2007* dialogue is opened.

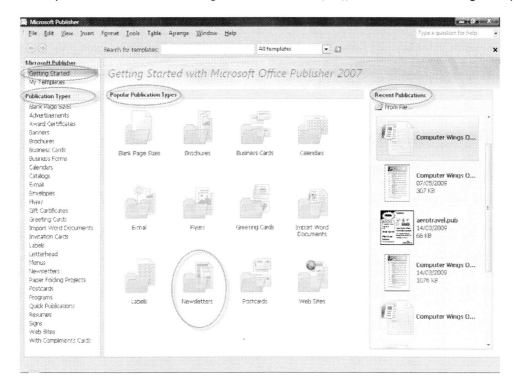

The Publisher environment consists of the following areas:

- A list of the most popular template types is displayed in the main area *Popular Publication Types*.

- A more extensive list is displayed in the navigation pane under *Publication Types*.

- Individual groups of templates are stored in each of the folders that you can access from either *Popular Publication Types* or *Publication Types*, eg Newsletters. Any *Recent Publications* files can be accessed by clicking on ⬛ From File... and navigating to the folder.

Opening a new document

You can open a new Publisher document using one of the templates available. A wide variety of communications material is available from business cards to newsletters and websites.

To open a new document based on a newsletter template:

1. Select *Newsletters* in the *Popular Publication Types* area.

Newsletters

2. The *Newsletters* folder is opened and your location is highlighted in the navigation pane.

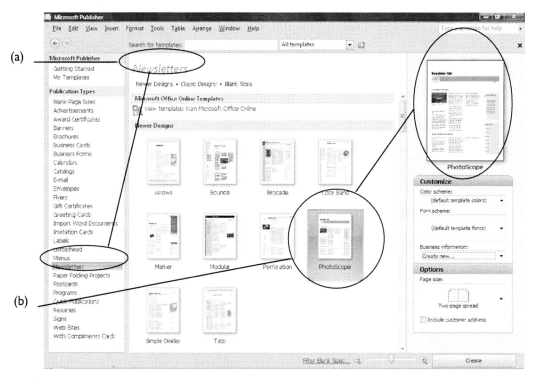

You can scroll up and down through the list available. Templates are grouped into categories such as *Newer Designs, Classic Designs, Blank Designs*. You can scroll through the list of available designs.

3. Select the format you want to use from those available. When you select a newsletter format such as *PhotoScope*, details about its format are displayed in the right hand pane.

4. Double-click to create a new document based on the selected format.

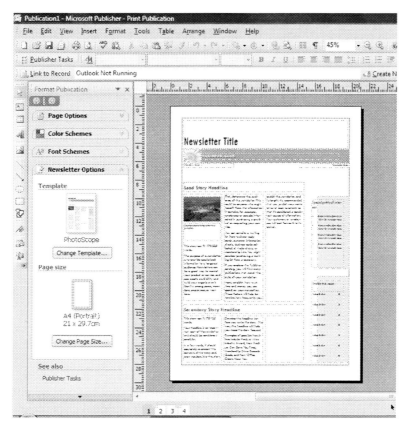

- Various formatting options are available and can be accessed from the *Format Publications* pane. You can open the various formatting options by selecting the individual tab. The tab opens and you can work with the formatting to suit your requirements.

- The main body contains the newsletter based on the selected formatting. You can alter the contents by clicking on an area and entering your new text. For example, you can change the heading title to reflect the content of the newsletter.

- You can switch to different pages in the newsletter by clicking on the page number in the bottom of the dialogue, where the current page is highlighted.

5. Select *Save As* from either the *File* menu or from the toolbar .

6. Specify a file name and select the folder where you want to store the file.

7. Select *Save*.

Files are automatically saved with the extension .pub and depending on your file settings the file extension may or may not show.

Closing a document

You should close your documents when you have finished working with them.

To close a document:

1. Select *Close* from the *File* menu, or press *Ctrl+F4*.

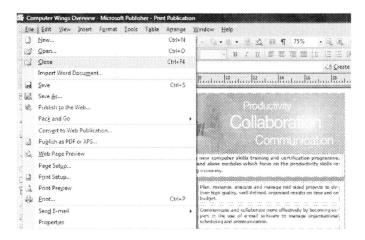

Closing Publisher

You can close Publisher directly from the *Getting Started* dialogue by selecting *Exit* from the *File* menu, or selecting *Alt+F4*.

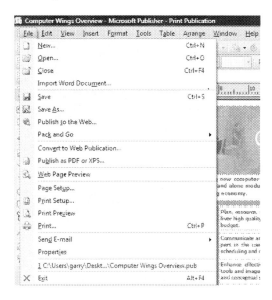

If you select to close Publisher while working with a template, you are requested to confirm whether or not you want to save your work. If you confirm by selecting *Yes*, you need to specify a file name for any open documents.

Layout

Depending on the type of document you wish to produce, Publisher provides various convenient layout templates, to allow you to layout your content effectively.

Working with page layouts

You can apply different page layouts to your project as follows:

1. Select *Blank Page Sizes* to open the menu of available blank page layouts.

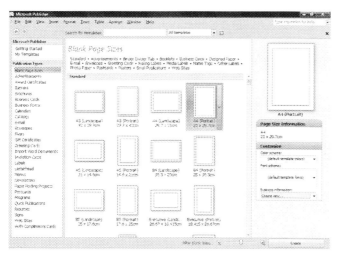

When you select a page, the page size information and other details are displayed in the right hand pane.

2. Double-click on the page size you require to create a new file based on the selected page size. A new document is created based on your page size selection.

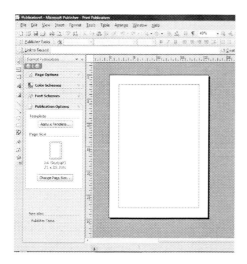

3. Either:

- Select *Apply a Template* to select from a list of available templates, or
- Use the features available in the *Options* toolbar to create your own design.

The example described here is based on using an available template.

4. Select *Apply a Template* to browse through the list of available templates:

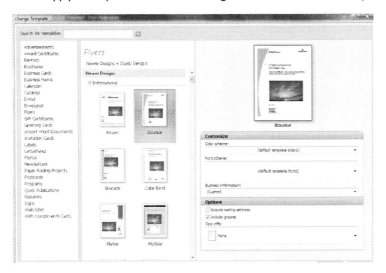

You can navigate through the available choices using the categories in the left hand navigation pane. When you select a template layout, additional details are displayed in the right hand pane.

5. Specify the brochure you want to use by either double-clicking on the brochure, or selecting the brochure and clicking *OK*.

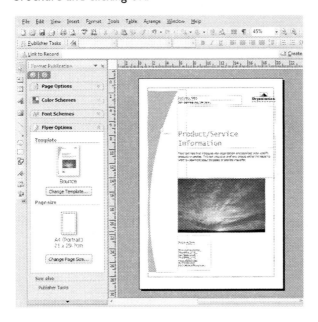

The format selected is applied to the blank page size.

You can now change the information as necessary to meet your requirements. When you are finished working, select *Save* and specify a new document name when prompted. Select *Close* to close the document.

Copying a layout

You can copy the layout from an existing document and apply it to a new document.

To copy a layout to a new document:

1. Open the document with the layout you want to copy.

2. Open the *Edit* menu and click on *Select All* or use the shortcut key *Ctrl+A*.

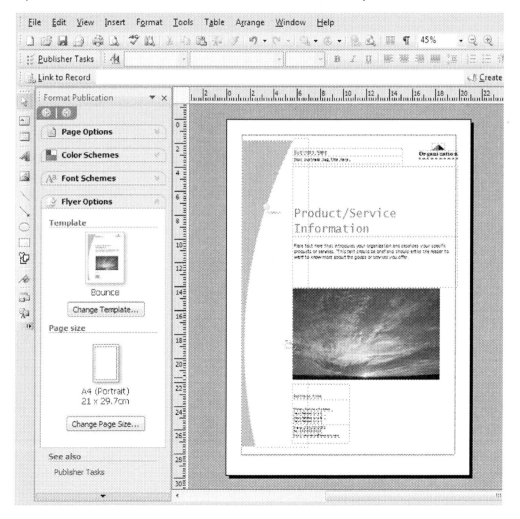

3. Select *Copy* from the *Edit* menu or use the shortcut *Ctrl+C*.

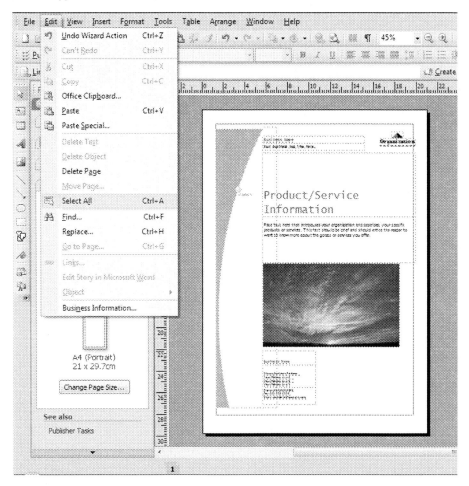

4. Select *New* from the *File* menu to create a new file. You are requested to select the publication type. Select *Blank Page Sizes* and select the page size you require. A new document is created based on your selection.

5. Select *Paste* from the *Edit* menu, or press *Ctrl+V* to apply the layout.

Deleting a layout

You can delete layouts or parts of layouts as required when working with a document.

To delete a layout:

1. Open the document with the layout you want to delete.

2. Open the *Edit* menu and click on *Select All* or use the shortcut key *Ctrl+A*.

3. Select *Delete* from your keyboard or select *Delete Objects* from the *Edit* menu.

View

Publisher contains a number of features for working effectively with documents. Once you have created a new document, you can then change the template, page size and other details associated with the layout.

Switching between layouts

Once you have selected a layout for your document, try out other layouts so that you can compare and select the best layout for your information. To switch between layouts:

1. Open the *Publications Options* in the *Format Publications* pane.

2. Select *Change Template*.

3. Navigate through the templates displayed, and double-click to select the template you want to use. Either double-click on the template, or select *OK*.

4. Select *Apply template to the current publication* and press *OK*.

The template is switched and the document is displayed with the new template applied. You can review whether this template meets your requirements and switch between other templates if required.

Activating an open project

When working with different files and file types, it is useful to switch between information or to minimise items that you do not require. You can activate files that you have minimised from the taskbar by double-clicking on the document.

When you are working with more than one document simultaneously, the total number of Publisher documents you are using is indicated and when you select the Publisher button, the individual file names are displayed.

Moving around a document

You can navigate to different pages in a document using the *Page Sorter* displayed in the bottom of the Publisher window.

To go to a different page in a document either:

- Select the page number using the Page Sorter, or

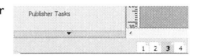

- Open the *Edit* menu and select *Go to Page*, or select *Ctrl+G*. The *Go To Page* dialogue is displayed and details the number of pages in the document. Specify the page you want to go to and select *OK*.

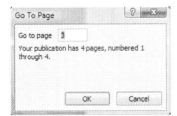

Displaying documents

When you work with Publisher you may need to manage more than one document at the same time.

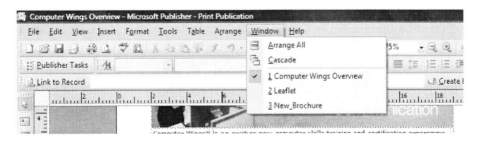

You can use different *Window* options as follows:

- Use the *Arrange All* option to display two or more documents simultaneously. You can compare the contents and layouts across the document set.

- Use the *Cascade* options to display all the open documents in a series on your screen. You can easily select individual documents as the individual window titles are based on the document names. As shown above, the title of the document is Computer Wings Overview.

You can use the options available from the *Taskbar* to organise how the various open documents are displayed. For example, if you want to display two or more windows vertically across the screen so that you can compare content and layout:

1. Open the documents you want to compare.

2. Close any other active windows.

3. Right-click in the taskbar to open the *Taskbar* menu.

4. Select *Show Windows Side by Side*.

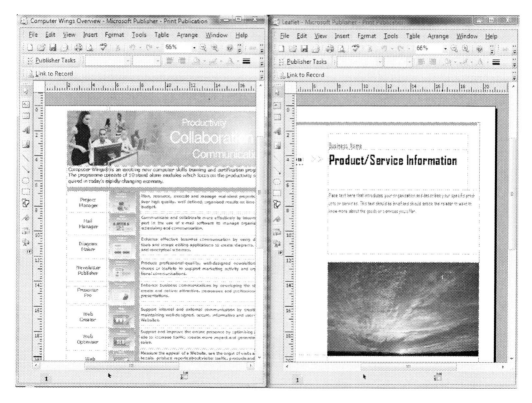

The documents are opened and you can compare the different layouts.

Using Zoom features

When you work with documents, it is often useful to enlarge and reduce the size of the information displayed. You can use the Zoom feature to select a display size suitable for the information. For example, if you are working with a large document, you will find it easier to work with smaller portions when editing text or imagery.

You can work with the Zoom options by either selecting the Zoom level you require:

- From the *View* menu, the *Zoom* levels available are displayed and you can select the level you want to use, or

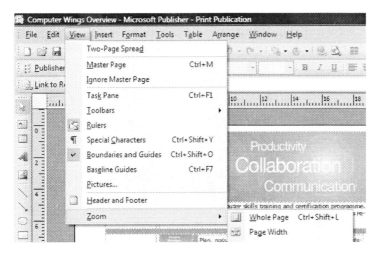

- Using the *Zoom* options on the *Standard* toolbar, you can select the *Zoom* level you require using either the percentage pulldown list to select the *Zoom* level, or using the ⊖ and ⊕ zoom buttons.

Save

To manage all your documents you will need to clearly identify and name your work, and then save your documents to a distinct folder for easy retrieval and use.

Save for the first time

You can save a document and any changes by selecting *Save* 💾 from either the *Standard* toolbar or the *File* menu:

- In a new document, you are prompted to specify a name for the document. Specify a file name (New_Style_Brochure_09) and select the folder. The file extension .pub is applied to any new file name.

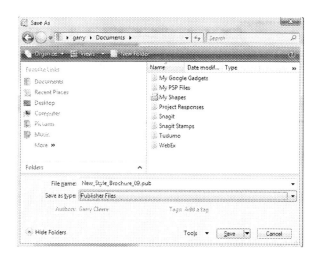

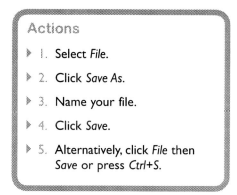

Actions

▶ 1. Select *File*.

▶ 2. Click *Save As*.

▶ 3. Name your file.

▶ 4. Click *Save*.

▶ 5. Alternatively, click *File* then *Save* or press *Ctrl+S*.

- In an existing document, the information is saved and you can either continue working with the document, or select *Close* to close the document.

Saving a new version

You can save a new version of an existing document by selecting *Save As*. You can specify a new file name to be used for the document and then press *Save*. The document is saved with the new file name and this name is displayed in the window title area.

Opening a saved file

You can open a file by either:

- Opening Publisher and selecting the file from the list of most recent documents you have worked with in the *Recent Publications* pane.

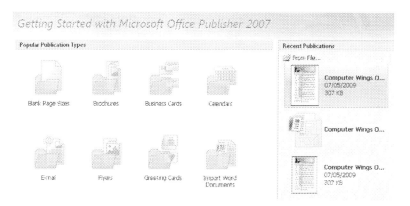

- Alternatively, select *Open* from *File* menu and navigate to the file you want to work with in the *Open Publication* dialogue. Once you have located and selected the file, select *OK*.

Quick Quiz

Select the correct answer from the following multiple-choice questions:

1   The *Getting Started* screen in Publisher allows you to choose from a number of which one of the following?

   a   Paper sizes

   b   Colour schemes

   c   Publication types

   d   Font styles

2   How many times may the layout of a publication be changed?

   a   Never

   b   Once only

   c   Once unless saved under a different name

   d   As many times as required

3   Which of the following is a shortcut to save the current publication file?

   a   *Ctrl+S*

   b   *Ctrl+C*

   c   *Ctrl+P*

   d   *Ctrl+F*

4   Which of the following commands splits the screen to show more than one publication?

   a   *View > Windows > Split*

   b   *View > Master Page*

   c   *Window > Arrange All*

   d   *Window > View > Split*

5   Which one of the following could not be produced using Publisher?

   a   Newsletter

   b   Spreadsheet

   c   Calendar

   d   Brochure

Answers to Quick Quiz

1   c   Publication types

2   d   As many times as required

3   a   *Ctrl+S*

4   c   *Window > Arrange All*

5   b   Spreadsheet

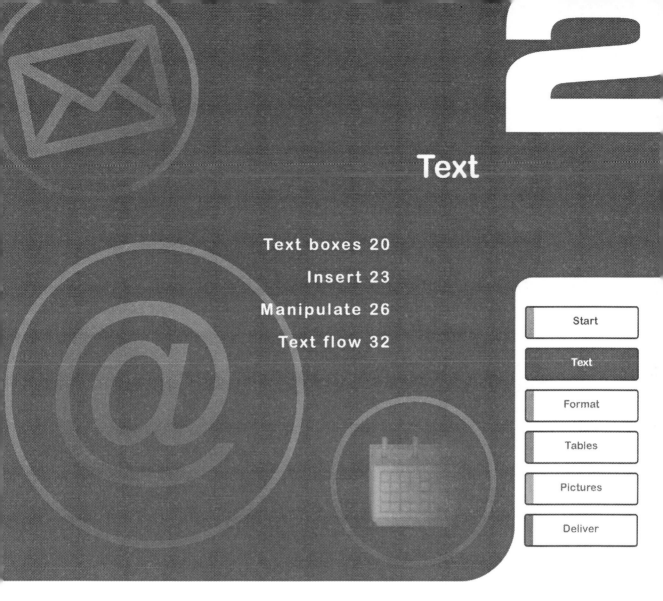

Text

Start
Text
Format
Tables
Pictures
Deliver

Measuring points

▸ Add a text box

▸ Move a text box manually, with precision

▸ Re-size a text box manually, with precision

▸ Insert text

▸ Select, delete text

▸ Drag and drop text

▸ Add text along a defined text path

▸ Recognise the text overflow symbol

▸ Add a border to a text box

▸ Position text in its text box

▸ Flip a text box

▸ Rotate a text box manually, with precision

▸ Change the text box vertical alignment

▸ Add columns in a text box

▸ Change text box gutter width

▸ Save text to a word processing file

▸ Import text

▸ Wrap text around a picture, text box

▸ Insert, delete pages

▸ Rearrange pages

▸ Drag, copy pages from another layout or project

▸ Link, unlink text boxes

▸ Delete text in a text box chain

▸ Unlink text in a text box chain

Introduction

Publisher has a range of tools to help present information. In this chapter text box manipulation and formatting, as well as linking text boxes is covered.

Text boxes

Text boxes are used in Publisher for holding text. The text box acts as a container for information. You can create as many text boxes as you need in a publication. Each text box can be handled uniquely allowing you to use many different styles for organising your information.

Once you have created a text box, you can move it anywhere in your publication. Additionally, you can assign different styles to individual text boxes.

Adding a text box

To add a text box:

1. Select *Text Box* from the *Insert* menu.

2. Click on the area in the document where you want to place the new text box and either:

   - Drag and drop the cursor as required to create a new text box to the required size, or

   - Begin entering information, a new text box containing the information entered is created.

Text boxes are highlighted with a dashed outline. When you select a text box, the various handle points (○) you can use for manipulating the text box are displayed.

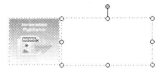

Moving text boxes

You can work with text boxes and position them manually or by using the menu options to position more precisely.

Manually

To manually move a text box:

1. Select the text box, grab anywhere on the text box outline.

2. Drag the text box to the new location and release.

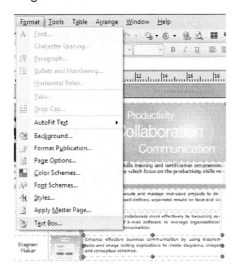

Precisely

1. Select the text box.

2. Select *Text Box* from the *Format* menu (The text box option is only displayed in the *Format* menu when a text box is selected).

3. Select the *Layout* tab to work with positioning options.

4. Specify the exact location for the text box using the *Horizontal* and *Vertical* scales. You can indicate using the options available whether the position is from the *Top Left Corner*, the *Center*, or from the *Top Right Corner*.

5. Select *OK*.

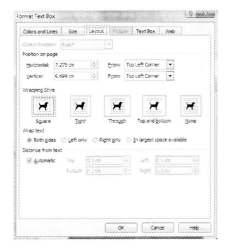

The text box is moved to the precise location.

Resizing text boxes

You can resize text boxes, for example, to accommodate certain types of texts such as headings. You can either manually resize text boxes, or use the layout options to precisely size a text box.

Manually

To manually resize a text box:

1. Select the text box.

2. Select a handle (○).

3. Drag the handle:

   - Inwards to reduce the text box size. The size of the new text area is displayed as you drag the selection point, or

   - Outwards to increase the text box size.

4. Release the cursor once the text box is the size you require.

You can repeat the steps to manipulate text boxes further if required.

Precisely

To resize a text box using precision:

1. Select the text box you want to resize.

2. Select *Text Box* from the *Format* menu.

3. Open the *Size* tab.

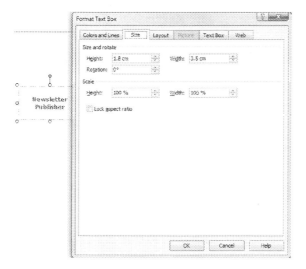

4. Specify the height and width you want to apply to the text box.

5. Select *OK*.

The size changes are applied to the text box.

Insert

Once you have designed your layout and decided on the template you want to use, you can begin to add content to your publication. You can also manipulate text to achieve different effects to enhance your communication.

Inserting text

When you are ready to start working on the content of your document, you can start inserting text.

To insert text in an open document:

1. Place the cursor in a text box and click.

   Your cursor begins to flash to indicate that you can begin inserting text.

2. When you have completed your text insertion, move the pointer outside the text area and click.

Deleting text

You can delete text by:

* Pressing the *Delete* key, or

* Selecting *Delete Text* from the *Edit* menu, or

- Right-clicking to open the *Object* menu and selecting either *Cut* or *Delete Text*.

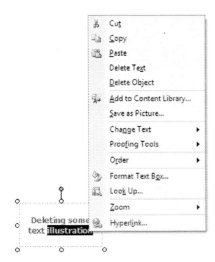

Moving text

You can quickly move around individual words or segments of text in a text box. To move a piece of text:

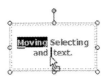

1. Select the piece of text you want to move.

2. Hold the left mouse key. A rectangle will be displayed under the cursor.

3. Drag the selected text to the new location and release the mouse key. The text is moved as required to the new location.

Aligning text

You can use the alignment features to vary the placement of text.

To specify how you want to align a piece of information:

1. Open the *Format Text Box* dialogue by either:

   - Right-clicking on the text box and selecting *Format Text Box*.

   - Opening the *Format* menu and selecting *Text Box*.

2. Open the *Text Box* tab to display the alignment options.

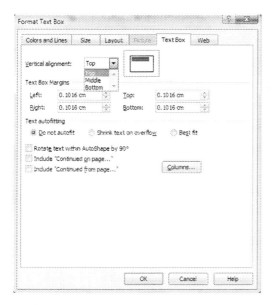

3. Click on the alignment options to display the options available, *Top, Middle and Bottom*. The option you select is reflected in the preview thumbnail.

4. Select *OK* to apply the format to the text box.

Text overflows

When you create text in a text box, sometimes the amount of information can exceed the space available. You are alerted to this with the overflow symbol ▣⋯ .

Once this symbol appears, you can review and either adjust the text box by resizing to accommodate the text or reduce the text content.

If you paste a large amount of information and exceed the text box space, the *AutoFlow* symbol is displayed and:

• If this is the first time the *AutoFlow* feature is being triggered, the following message is displayed:

- Select *Yes* if you want to use the *AutoFlow* feature to flow text into existing boxes.

- If you want to retain control, select *No* so that you can manually work with various segments of text in the various text boxes.

- The following message is displayed when you select *Yes* and if the *AutoFlow* feature is triggered again:

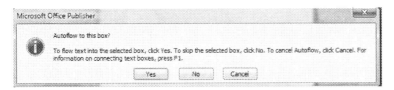

Select *Yes* if you want to use the *AutoFlow* feature for positioning your text.

Manipulate

You can arrange and position text boxes so that information can be presented appropriately. For example, if you want to highlight a piece of information, you can easily draw a border around it to separate it from the main body of text.

Adding borders

Borders are a useful way to arrange and organise textual information. By using borders you can emphasise, distinguish or relate different ideas or concepts.

To add a border to a text box:

1. Select a text box.

2. Open the *Format Text Box* dialogue by either:

   - Right-clicking on the text box and selecting *Format Text Box*.

   - Opening the *Format* menu and selecting the text box.

   The *Format Text Box* dialogue is displayed:

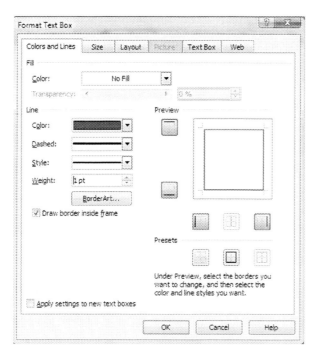

Use the options available to:

- Define the colour and any other features you want applied to the line.
- Select an available preset so that either a single line is applied, or to surround the text box as shown.

Any line formatting you select is displayed in the *Preview* area.

3. Select *OK* to apply changes to the selected text box.

Positioning text

You can specify whether you want text to be automatically fitted within a text box or if you want to manually control how text fits.

Automatically

To automatically adjust text so that it fits in a text box:

1. Select a text box.

2. Select *AutoFit Text* from the *Format* menu. The list of available options is displayed:

- Select *Best Fit* if you want text size increased or reduced when you resize a text box, or
- *Shrink Text On Overflow* if you want text to be reduced to prevent overflow.

Manually

You can adjust text manually by selecting the text and opening the *Font* dialogue box (select *Font* from the *Format* menu). For example, open the *Font* dialogue and select the font you want to use, the style you want to apply to the font, and the font size.

Adjusting alignment and line spacing

You can adjust the line spacing and text alignment in a text box by:

1. Selecting a text box.

2. Select *Paragraph* from the *Format* menu.

3. Open the *Indents* and *Spacing* tab.

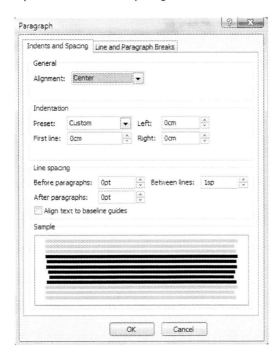

Choose:

- The alignment you require from the list available.

- Any indention you want to apply.

- The line spacing you want to apply including the spacing between lines of text.

    A preview of how text will appear is displayed in the *Sample* area.

4. Select *OK* to accept the formatting and to apply it to the selected text.

Flip, rotate text boxes

You can manipulate text boxes using the *Rotate* or *Flip* options so that information can be presented at different angles.

Rotating text boxes

You can rotate text boxes:

- Manually by dragging the text box handle ( ). Select the top circle of the handle. The cursor changes to circular symbol ( ). Click on the symbol and rotate the text box to the required position.

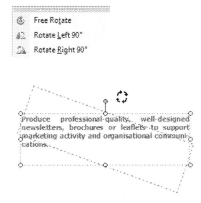

Flipping text boxes

You can flip text boxes:

- By using *Flip* options available from the *Arrange* menu to flip the text.

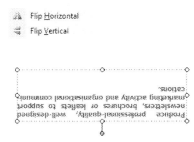

Change vertical alignment

For flexibility and presentation, Publisher assists in presenting text at *Top*, *Middle* or *Bottom* of the text box.

To change vertical alignment, select the text box:

1. Click *Format*.

2. Click *Text Box*.

3. Select the *Text Box* tab.

4. Select the alignment you require in the *Vertical Alignment* list.

5. Click *OK*.

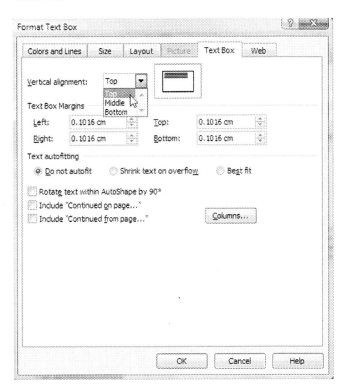

Adding columns

You can use columns to organise information in a text box.

To add columns:

1. Open the *Format Text Box* dialogue by either:

    *   Right-clicking on the text box and selecting *Format Text Box*, or

    *   Opening the *Format* menu and selecting *Text Box*.

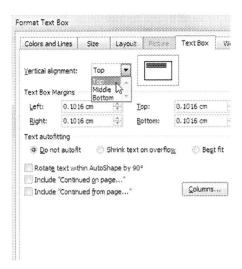

2. Open the *Text Box* tab and select *Columns*.

3. In the *Columns* dialogue, specify the number of columns and the spacing between the columns. A preview is displayed showing how the information will appear.

4. Select *OK* to apply the format to the text box.

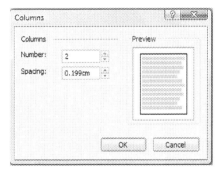

Column gutters

The space between columns is called the gutter. You can adjust the space between columns in the *Columns* dialogue. Simply choose the number of columns required and adjust the gutter spacing width as necessary.

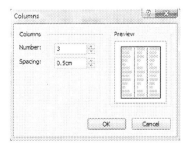

Output to a word processing file

You can save the contents of a publication to a word processing file, this can be useful to share and exchange work with colleagues.

To save the text from a publication to a word file:

1. Open the publication.

2. Select *Save As* from the *File* menu.

3. Specify the file type associated with your word processing application. Open the *Save as type* list to display the list of file types available. Use the scroll bar to navigate to a specific file type.

4. Specify a file name.

5. Select *Save*. A message is displayed informing you that the file type selected only supports text and asks you to confirm that you want to save a text only version of the information from the selected document.

6. Confirm that you want to continue by selecting *OK*.

Text Flow

Sometimes when working in Publisher you will need to bring in text from other applications such as a word processer. Publisher has a range of features to help incorporate text from other applications.

Importing text

You can import text from another application such as Word to use in your Publisher document.

You can import text as follows:

1. Select *Import Word Documents* either from the:

    *   *Publication Types* page when you open Publisher or when you create a new document.

- File menu for importing text into an existing document.

2. Select a format type to use in the *Import Word Documents* pane.

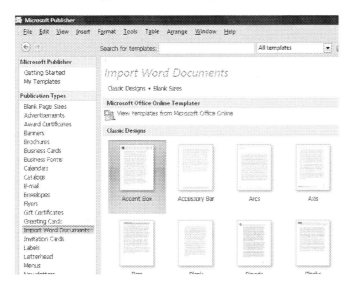

To select a format type, either select a format type and press *Create*, or double-click on the format type.

3. When the text import is complete, check the information to ensure the integrity of the transferred information.

Wrapping text

When you work with print type material, you have a variety of options available such as wrapping text around a graphic so that the graphic and the text are an integral unit of information. While this type of formatting is useful when working with documents, it does not automatically transfer when working with web material. If you create information for a website based on a print publication, any formatting around graphics is lost.

You can specify how you want your text to appear in relation to an associated graphic.

To organise how you want text to flow:

1. Select the picture.

2. Open the *Format Picture* dialogue by either:

   • Selecting *Picture* from the *Format* menu, or

   • Right-click on the picture and selecting *Format Picture*.

3. Select the *Layout* tab.

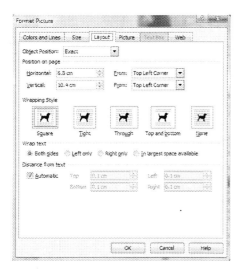

Specify the wrapping style you want to apply, and where applicable, how you want to wrap text around the selected picture.

Publisher has a range of text wrap styles:

   • *Square*

   • *Tight*

   • *Through*

4. Select *OK* to apply.

The following examples illustrate some common text wrapping options:

Square wrapping

When you select the *Square* wrapping style, information is wrapped around the picture. However, you can also select this option if you only want to wrap text on a specific side, for example, on the left side.

You can use the *Distance from text* options to specify any specific spacing you want to apply between the text and the graphic.

Tight wrapping

When you use the *Tight* wrapping style, text is also wrapped around the picture as with the square style, but there is spacing applied from the picture frame.

The *Distance from text* feature is not available when you select this style as text is aligned as tightly as possible to the picture.

Top and bottom wrapping

When you select the *Top and bottom* wrapping style, your text is only displayed at the top and bottom as shown in this example.

Inserting pages

You can add one or more pages to a document.

To add pages:

1. Select *Page* from the *Insert* menu or press *Ctrl+Shift+N*. The *Insert Page* dialogue is displayed:

Specify the number of new pages you want to add to the document and whether you want the new pages in front of or behind the current page. You can specify whether you want any new pages created to be:

- blank

- contain a text box

- duplicate all the objects on an existing page in the document by specifying *Duplicate all objects on page*.

2. Select *OK*. The document is displayed and the *Page Sorter* is updated with any additional page numbering.

Deleting pages

To delete a page from a publication:

1. Open a publication and either:

- Select *Delete page* from the *Edit* menu while the page is opened.

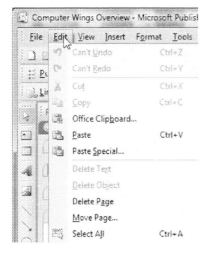

- Right-click on the page you want to delete in *Page Sorter* menu, and select *Delete Page*.

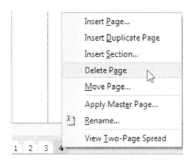

2.   Select *Yes* to confirm that you want to delete the page when the following message is displayed:

Reorganising pages

You can reorganise your publication to reflect changes in structure and presentation of material. For example, if you want to change the location of certain information, you can quickly move the pages around using the *Page Sorter*. To move pages using the *Page Sorter*:

1.   Click on the page you want to move, for example, to move page 3 so that it becomes page 2, click on page 3.

2.   Drag and drop the page ⬚ to the new location as indicated with the symbol (▼).

You can view documents over a two page spread by either selecting:

- Two *Page Spread* from the *View* menu.

- View *Two-Page Spread* from the *Page Sorter* menu.

When you reorganise pages using two page spread, the *Page Sorter* indicates that you are using a two page spread.

Copying pages between publications

Once you have created information, you can reuse it in other publications by using the copy and paste tools.

To copy and paste information between two publications:

1. Open the page from which you want to copy information.

2. Select the information you want to copy. If you want to copy:

    - The complete layout applied to a page:

        1. Choose *Select All* (or press *Ctrl+A*) from the *Edit* menu.

        2. Select *Copy (Ctrl+C)* from the *Edit* menu.

    - A portion of text from a page: highlight the text and choose *Copy* from the *Edit* menu (or press *Ctrl+C*).

3. Go to the new publication and select *Paste* from the *Edit* menu or press *Ctrl+V*.

The selected information is copied to the target document.

Linking and unlinking text boxes

You can create links between text boxes to associate and group information using the *Connect Text Boxes* toolbar.

This toolbar contains the following options:

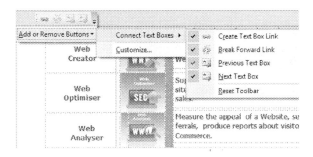

If the *Connect Text Boxes* toolbar is not displayed, you can select it from the *Toolbars* list in the *View* menu.

To create a connection between text boxes:

1. Select a text box.

2. Select the *Create Text Box Link* button.

3. Move the pointer which is now changed to a pitcher to the empty text box to which you want to create a connection. The pitcher symbol changes to the image of a pitcher being poured This symbol is only displayed when you are able to create the connection. Otherwise the pitcher remains upright.

4. Right-click to create the connection.

5. You can repeat the above steps to link additional text boxes.

You can navigate between connected text boxes using either the:

- Go to *Next Text Box* or the *Go to Previous Text Box* symbols displayed next to the text box.

- *Next Text Box* or the *Previous Text Box* buttons from the *Create Text Box Link* toolbar.

Unlinking text in a text box chain

You can also break a link between text boxes and reduce the extent of the text box chain. To unlink a text box, select the text box and select the *Break forward Link* button.

Deleting text from chain

To delete text in a text box chain, select a text box in the chain and either select *Cut* from the *Edit* menu or press *Ctrl+X*.

Quick Quiz

Select the correct answer from the following multiple-choice questions:

1   You have just connected two text boxes. What does this allow you to do?

    a   Format text in both boxes identically

    b   Duplicate text in both text boxes

    c   Create columns of different widths

    d   Move overflow text into another text box

2   Which of the following is a text wrapping option in Publisher?

    a   Loose

    b   Centered

    c   Round

    d   Tight

3   Which of the following menu command sequences inserts new pages into a publication?

    a   *Edit > Page > Insert*

    b   *Arrange > Insert > Page*

    c   *Insert > Page*

    d   *View > New Page*

4   The green circle on a selected text box can be used to perform which one of the following?

    a   Move the box

    b   Resize the box

    c   Rotate the box

    d   Delete the box

5   Which of the following is a keyboard shortcut used to cut text?

    a   *Ctrl+D*

    b   *Ctrl+X*

    c   *Ctrl+C*

    d   *Ctrl+V*

Answers to Quick Quiz

1	d	Move overflow text into another text box
2	d	Tight
3	c	*Insert > Page*
4	c	Rotate the 60x
5	b	*Ctrl+X*

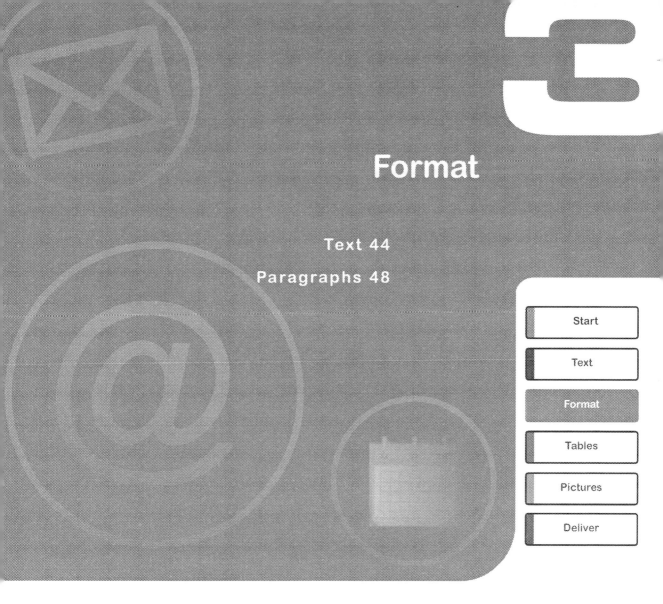

Format

Text 44

Paragraphs 48

Start	
Text	
Format	
Tables	
Pictures	
Deliver	

Measuring points

- Change the font size, colour of text
- Change style of text in a text box
- Re-size type
- Change text leading
- Kern text
- Indent first line of a paragraph

- Create a new paragraph
- Change spacing between paragraphs
- Apply a soft paragraph return
- Copy formats in the same project
- Create, or edit hyphenation, justification

Introduction

Colour, size, type and styles all add to the visual appeal of your publication. This chapter describes how you work with some of the features of formatting. Using the various formatting options, you can apply different styles to the content of your documents. The formatting features allow you to specify various features such as applying kerning when working with text or pictures. It is good practice to make design choices about your font size and colour at the very beginning of your document.

Text

Font size and colour

To change the font applied to a piece of text, select your text and go to the *Format* menu and select *Font*:

- Change the font attributes including the font by selecting the options you want to apply from the various lists such as *Font style* and *Size*.

- Specify any effects you want to apply to the text by selecting one of the options available such as *Outline*.

- Review your selection in the *Sample*:

  1. Select *Apply*, your changes are applied to the selected text.

  2. Select *OK* to accept your changes or *Cancel* to close the *Font* dialogue without making any changes.

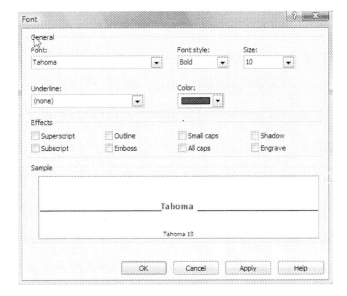

Change styles

You can use styles to define the formatting for various elements such as headings and body text.

To apply a style:

1.   Select the text to which you want to apply a style.

2.   Open the *Styles* pane by either:

   •   Selecting *Styles* from the *Format* menu, or

   •   Opening the *Format Publication* menu and selecting *Styles*. The list of available styles is displayed in the navigation panes.

3.   Select a style from the list to apply to the selected text.

Resizing text

You can use the features available with Publisher to resize text to fit within text boxes.

To resize text:

1. Select a text box.

2. Open the *Autofit Text* options available from the *Format* menu.

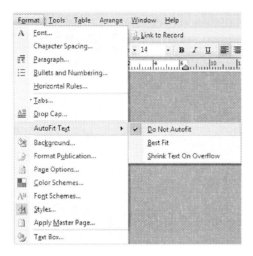

3. Select the option you want to use:

    *   *Do Not Autofit* if you do not want to use the Publisher features available.
    *   *Best Fit* if you want text automatically resized to fit the selected text box.
    *   *Shrink Text On Overflow* to reduce text size if text overflows from the selected text box.

Changing text leading

Text leading refers to the spacing between lines of text.

You can vary the line spacing applied to text as follows:

1. Select the text you want to alter.

2. Open the *Paragraph* dialogue by either selecting *Paragraph* from the *Format* menu, or by clicking on the *Line Spacing* button.

3. Open the *Indents and Spacing* tab.

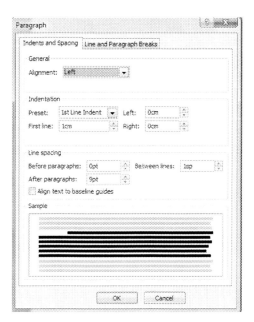

Specify the line spacing you want to apply to the selected text.

You can specify the spacing you want to apply:

- Before and after any paragraph, for example, you can specify that you want to apply 3pt before a paragraph and 1pt after a paragraph.

- Between lines, for example, 1pt.

4. Select *OK* when you have completed your changes.

Kern text

Kerning is used to specify letter spacing. The space between letters can be adjusted and space added or subtracted. You can use kerning to make your text more appealing or readable.

To apply kerning:

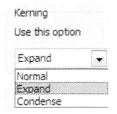

1. Select the two characters you wish to change.

2. Select *Format* menu, click *Character Spacing*.

3. Under *Kerning,* click *Expand* or *Condense* to adjust spacing, and then enter an amount between 0 points and **600** points in the *By this amount box.*

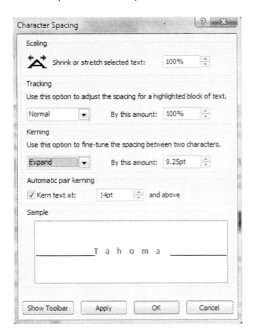

The rest of the text is the same. You can preview the kerning selected in the *Sample* area. In this example, the text is to be expanded with spacing of 9.25 points.

4. Select *Apply* to apply your changes to the selected text.

5. Select *OK* to complete.

Paragraphs

You can apply different styles to paragraphs to clearly signify the beginning and end of pieces of text.

Using indents

You can indent the first line of a paragraph as follows:

1. Select a paragraph or text box in your publication.

2. Click on *Paragraph* from the *Format* menu.

3. In the *Paragraph* dialogue box, specify the indentation you want to apply. For example, you want to indent the first line by 1sp (cm) as specified here:

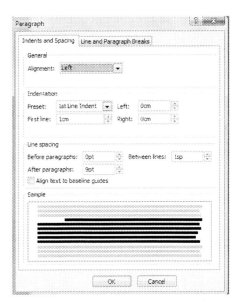

4.   Select *OK* to close and return to your publication.

Creating new paragraphs

To create a new paragraph in a text box, place the cursor at the end of a piece of text and press *Enter*. The cursor begins a new paragraph on the next line. You can change the spacing before and after paragraphs using the line spacing options in the *Paragraph* dialogue.

Paragraph spacing

You can change the spacing between paragraphs, for example, when starting new topics.

To specify the line spacing you want to apply to a document:

1. Select the text or text box.

2. Click on *Paragraph* from the *Format* menu.

3. Open the *Indents and Spacing* tab.

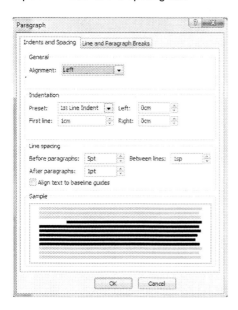

Specify the spacing you want to apply before and any spacing you want to apply after the paragraph. In this example, you want to apply 5pt spacing before a paragraph and 1pt after the paragraph.

You can preview your changes in the *Sample* area.

4. Select *OK*. Your changes are applied to the selected paragraph or any paragraphs in the selected text box.

Apply a soft paragraph return

A soft return inserts a line break without a paragraph break. They are used for example when entering address information. To apply a soft return when working with text, place your cursor at the point where you want to apply a paragraph and press *Shift+Enter*. The cursor shifts to the beginning of the next line.

Copy formats

You can copy the format you have applied from a piece of text to another piece of text.

To copy a format:

1. Select the text that is based on the format you want to copy.

2. Click on *Format Painter* from the *Standard* Toolbar:

> The cursor is changed to the paintbrush symbol ▲ representing *Format Painter*.

3. Drag the cursor over the text you want to change.

> Formatting text
>
> ▲ **Formatting text**

4. Release the cursor to finish.

Setting hyphenation styles

You can set the style rules you want to apply to the use of hyphenation. You can, for example, specify that you do not want text to be automatically hyphenated.

To set the type of hyphenation you want to use:

1. Open the *Tools* menu.

2. Click on *Language* and select *Hyphenation* or use the shortcut *Ctrl+Shift+H*.

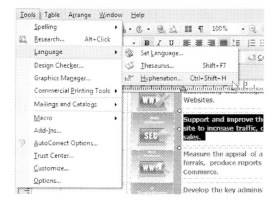

3. Set your preferences in the *Hyphenation* dialogue.

Automatically

- Text maybe automatically hyphenated, *Automatically hyphenate* this story.

- Hyphenation may be triggered when text is within 0.635cm of the right margin.

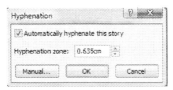

4. Set preferences as required.

5. Select *OK* to confirm.

Manually

If you want to manually set how a word is hyphenated, select *Manually* from the *Hyphenation* dialogue. You can specify where exactly you want hyphenation to occur in your text.

Using justification

Justification defines how you want text aligned on the right and left margins.

To set the justification for a piece of text:

1. Select the text.

2. Select the justification you want to apply from the *Toolbar* menu.

Select:

Left: to align text with the left margin (*Ctrl+L*).

Center: to align text on both sides of the center (*Ctrl+C*).

Right: to align text on the right margin (*Ctrl+R*).

Justified: to align text with both the left and right margins (*Ctrl+J*).

Quick Quiz

Select the correct answer from the following multiple-choice questions:

1   Which of the following is an option on the *AutoFit Text* menu?

     a   *Best Fit*

     b   *Character spacing*

     c   *Increase*

     d   *Expand*

2   Adjusting the space between text characters is called?

     a   Tracking

     b   Banking

     c   Filling

     d   Kerning

3   What does the *Format Painter* tool do? Choose one from the following:

     a   Applies larger font sizing to text selection

     b   Copies formatting from an initial text selection to a new selection

     c   Removes all formatting from text

     d   Deletes all new text selections

4   Which key combination gives what is known as a 'soft' paragraph return?

     a   *Shift+Enter*

     b   *Ctrl+Enter*

     c   *Alt+Enter*

     d   *Alt Gr+Enter*

Answers to Quick Quiz

1   a   *Best Fit*

2   d   Kerning

3   a   Copies formatting from an initial text selections to a new selection

4   d   *Shift+Enter*

Tables

Insert 56

- Start
- Text
- Format
- **Tables**
- Pictures
- Deliver

Measuring points

▶ Add a table
▶ Add, edit, and remove text in a table
▶ Resize a column or row
▶ Change the border colour, styles in a table

▶ Change the background colour of a table, cells
▶ Add, delete rows or columns
▶ Make cells or columns of consistent size
▶ Merge cells in a table

Introduction

Tables help organise and present information clearly and logically. Different table styles are available within Publisher to create a table layout to suit your publication. This chapter covers creating, formatting and manipulating tables.

Insert

Tables allow your audience to easily take in logical information and are an important communication technique in any publication.

Adding table

To add a table in a publication:

1. Open the *Table* menu and click on *Insert* or click on the *Insert Table* button.

2. Select *Table*. The *Create Table* dialogue is displayed, choose:

   - The number of rows and columns you want in your table.

   - Whether or not you want a table format applied. Select a *Table format* or select *[None]* if you do not want a format applied.

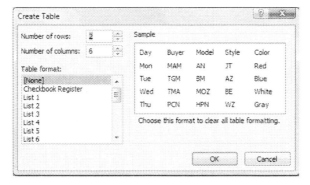

3. Click *OK*.

Choose a table format

The various table formats are displayed in the *Table format* list. When you select a format, a preview of the selected format is displayed in the *Sample* with a message suggesting how the format can be applied. These table formats provide you with standard designs that you can quickly apply when creating a table.

 Once you have created a table you can apply a whole range of pre-defined styles using *Table AutoFormat* from the *Table* menu.

In this example, the *Table format* selected is *List I* with the message *Use this format for making comparisons or lists.*

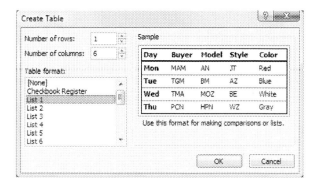

The *Sample* displays a preview of the table style applied with this table format such as any row and column borders and any highlighting applied.

 If you wish to quickly navigate throughout the cells in the table, use the *TAB* key.

Add text in a table

Once you have designed your table, you can add text to the individual cells. To add information to a table, click inside the cell and add information by either typing directly or pasting information into the cell. Once you have created information in a cell; you can work with the information in the same way as with other text in your document.

Resizing columns and rows

You can resize columns and rows based on your design requirements.

To resize a table row or column:

1. Click on the row or column you want to adjust.

2. Drag and release the cursor to the new column width or row height.

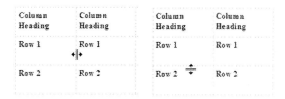

Table borders

To add a border to a table:

1. Select the table.

2. Open the *Format Table* dialogue box by either:

    *   Right-clicking on the text box and selecting *Format Table*.

    *   Opening the *Format* menu and selecting *Table*.

    The *Format Table* dialogue box is displayed:

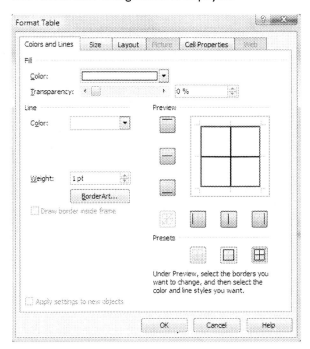

    Use the options available to:

    *   Define the colour applied to any lines.

    *   Select an available preset to apply borders as required to your table.

    Any line formatting you select is displayed in the *Preview* area.

3. Select *OK* to apply changes to the selected text box.

Background colour

To set a background colour for a table:

1. Select the table.

2. Open the *Format Table* dialogue box.

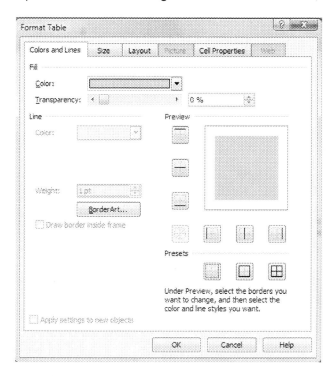

Use the options available to:

- Define the fill colour from the list available in the colour list.
- Select if you want to change the colour of any table lines.

Your changes are displayed in the *Preview* area.

3. Select *OK* to apply changes to the selected text box.

Rows and columns

To add a row or a column to a table:

1. Select a cell in your table.

2. Open *Insert* from the *Table* menu.

3. Select whether you want to insert a row or column in your table and whether you want the:

- Column inserted to the left or right of the selected cell.
- Row inserted above or below the selected cell.

To delete a row or a column:

1. Select a cell in your table.

2. Open the *Table* menu.

3. Select whether you want to delete a row or column in your table.

Column size

You can use the *AutoFormat* feature to apply a pre-defined standard format to a table:

1. Select the table.

2. Click on *Table AutoFormat* from the *Table* menu.

3. In the *Auto Format* dialogue, specify the table format you want to apply to your table from the list available.

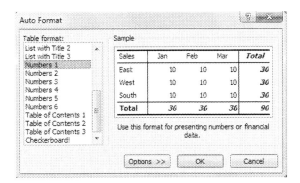

A preview of the text formatting is displayed in the sample area.

4. Select *OK* when you have chosen a format.

Merging cells

You can merge two or more cells in a table. This is useful where you need to vary the size to accommodate table headings.

To merge cells in a table:

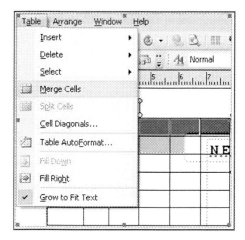

1. Select two or more cells that you want to merge.

2. Select *Merge Cells* from the *Table* menu.

The selected cells are merged. Any existing text is appended together in the single merged cell.

Quick Quiz

Select the correct answer from the following multiple-choice questions:

1   You wish to quickly move the cursor throughout a table using a keyboard stroke. Which key will allow you to do this?

    a   *TAB*

    b   *Enter*

    c   *Shift*

    d   *Space*

2   You want some of the cells in your table to enlarge in line with text entry in the cells. Which menu command will allow you to do this?

    a   *Expand to fit text*

    b   *Grow to fit text*

    c   *Autofit text*

    d   *Manual fit text*

3   You want entered text in your table to display in the centre of the cell. Which command sequence will allow you to do this?

    a   *Format Table > Cell Properties*

    b   *Format Table > Size*

    c   *Format Table > Layout*

    d   *Format Table > Web*

4   You wish to apply a pre-defined format approach to your table. Which *Table* menu command will allow you to do this?

    a   *New Format*

    b   *Format TableNew*

    c   *Pre Format*

    d   *Table AutoFormat*

Answers to Quick Quiz

1   a   *TAB*

2.   b   *Grow to fit text*

3   a   *Format Table > Cell Properties*

4   d   *Table AutoFormat*

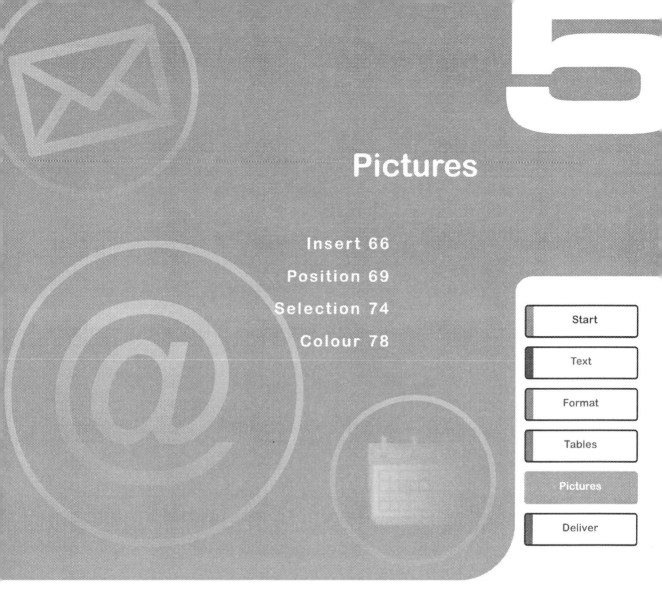

Pictures

Start

Text

Format

Tables

Pictures

Deliver

Measuring points

▸ Add a picture box
▸ Import a picture in different formats
▸ Recognise different picture formats and their characteristics
▸ Resize a picture box manually, with precision
▸ Delete a picture box, delete picture only
▸ Copy a picture box
▸ Move a picture box manually, with precision
▸ Scale, centre a picture in a picture box
▸ Crop a picture within its picture box
▸ Rotate, skew a picture

▸ Flip a picture
▸ Select all items in page, project
▸ Select, de-select multiple items
▸ Copy, move items within a page, between projects
▸ Group, ungroup items
▸ Remove an item from a group
▸ Promote, demote items
▸ Change a background colour
▸ Change colour in a picture
▸ Change the colour of a text box border

Introduction

Pictures are a powerful tool in the presentation of information. You should ensure however, that the images you include in your information are relevant and do not distract from your message.

Pictures also provide a means to explain a concept or a process graphically. They can present information more clearly than text. This chapter explains how you work with pictures in Publisher. Both basic tasks, such as inserting a picture in a file, to more complex features such as making format changes, are covered.

Insert

Picture frames allow you to precisely position and present images and graphics within your document. Publisher has many tools to help you work with images.

Adding a picture box

To add a picture from the Clip Art library to a publication select *Insert*, click *Picture* and select *Clip Art*, or:

1. Open the *Clip Art* in the *Publisher Tasks* pane.

    a. Click on the *Other Task Panes* button ▼ to display the list of task panes.

    b. Select *Clip Art*.

        The Clip Art Catalogue is opened.

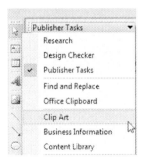 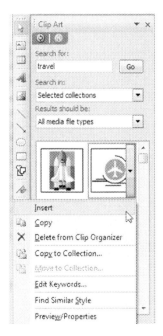

2. Select *Empty Picture Frame* button from the *Object* toolbar. (You can also open the *Insert* menu, select *Picture* and select *Empty Picture Frame* from the list displayed).

3. Navigate to the picture you want to insert from Clip Art catalogue.

4. Click on the picture and select the arrow ▼ to open the picture menu.

5. Select *Insert* and the picture is added.

Using different picture formats

You can import pictures stored in a range of formats. To insert a picture based on a different format in a publication:

1. Select *Picture from file* either from the *Objects* toolbar or from the *Insert > Pictures* menu.

2. Select a specific picture file type. You can scroll through the list available. When you select a specific file type such as JPEG File Interchange Format (.jpg), any file with the file extensions, .jpg, .jpeg, .jfif, .jpe is displayed in the file list.

3. Select the picture file you want to insert.

4. Select *Insert*.

The picture file is inserted in your document.

About different picture formats

Different picture formats are based on different features. When creating a publication, you should select a format that meets the requirements of your communications medium.

File formats define standardised methods for organising and storing images. The image quality depends upon the file format used to store the image data.

The following describes the main features of some of the more common picture formats:

Format	Extensions	Description
Joint Photographic Experts Group (JPEG)	.jpg, .jpeg, .jfif, .jpe, .jif	JPEG is the most commonly used compression method for photographic images. The compression level used for storing an image is reflected in the image quality. JPEGs can achieve a 10:1 compression ratio with an acceptable quality level. However, repeated editing and saving causes jpeg images to degrade in quality.
Graphic Interchange Format (GIF)	.gif	The GIF format supports 256 colours based on an Format (GIF) 8-bit palette. It is most suitable for storing simple graphics such as shapes, and logos. This file format supports animation and is widely used to provide image animation effects. It is widely used in graphics, particularly animation, on the Web.
Portable Network Graphics (PNG)	.png	This format is a patent-free (open source) replacement of the GIF format. It supports true colour (16 million colours). It was designed as a patent less replacement of the GIF while also aiming to replace and improve upon the GIF format.
Windows bitmap (BMP)	.bmp	The BMP image file format is used for storing bitmap digital images particularly on the Microsoft Windows Operating System.
Tagged Image File (TIFF)	.tif, .tiff	TIFF is use for storing images including photographs and line art. It is a flexible file format for handling images and data in a single file. TIFF files are the preferred photographic standard of the printing industry. However, as it is not widely supported by web browsers, it should not be used for related material.

Position

Publisher picture frame tools also allow you to resize, delete, copy, move, scale, crop, rotate and flip pictures.

Resizing pictures

You can resize pictures that you have included in your publications.

You can either resize a picture manually or precisely define your sizing requirements.

Manually

1. Select the picture frame.

2. Select a handle (○).

3. Click and hold the handle to adjust the size as required.

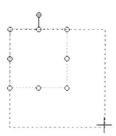

4. Release when you have achieved the required size.

The picture frame is resized to the specified size.

Precisely

1. Select the picture you want to resize.

2. Select *Picture* from the *Format* menu.

3. Open the *Size* tab.

4. Specify the height and width you want to apply to the picture, or use the *Scale* feature to resize a picture to a specific percentage.

Deleting pictures

You may not always wish to keep the image you import or copy into your document. You can easily delete an image.

To delete a picture:

1. Select the picture frame.

2. Press the *Delete* key.

Copying a picture

To copy a picture:

1. Select the picture frame.

2. Right-click to open the *Object* menu.

3. Select *Copy*.

4. Place the cursor at the point where you want to insert the copy of the picture.

5. Right-click again to open the *Object* menu and select *Paste*.

Moving a picture

You can move picture boxes either manually or precisely.

Manually

1. Select the picture.

2. Right-click and then hold to move the picture to the new location.

3. Release the mouse button. The picture is moved to the new location in your publication.

Precisely

1. Select the picture.

2. Right-click to open the objects menu and select *Format Picture*.

3. Select that you want the placement to be *exact*.

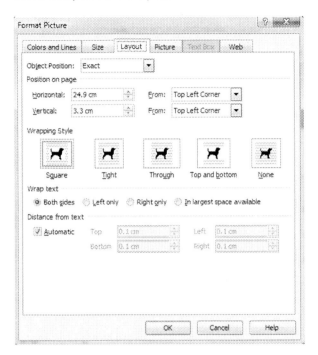

4. Specify where the picture should be located in the current publication.

Scaling pictures

You can scale images in a picture box so that the image is rescaled proportionally.

To scale an image:

1. Select the image you want to rescale.

2. Select and hold the cursor.

3. Drag to reduce the size as required to fit.

4. Release the cursor.

The whole picture is resized to the required scale.

Cropping pictures

You can crop a picture to display a particular piece of information.

To crop a picture:

1. Select the picture frame.

2. Select *Crop* ⊢ from the *Picture* toolbar.

3. Select the edge or corners from which you want to crop the picture and drag and drop the cursor. A heavy dashed outline is displayed around the picture. Select the points at which you want to perform the crop and drag the cursor. You can select any of the borders and corners.

4. When complete, click outside the picture to deselect the picture. Only the cropped image is now displayed.

Rotate, flip a picture

Rotate a picture

To rotate a picture, select the picture and click the green circle at the top of the picture and press the left mouse button to rotate the picture.

This can also be done using the *Arrange* menu.

Flip a picture

To flip a picture:

1.   Select the picture.

2.   Open the *Arrange* menu and select *Rotate or Flip*.

3.   Select whether you want to flip the selected picture horizontally or vertically.

     The picture is flipped based on your selection.

Selection

Often when working in Publisher you need to manipulate and arrange numerous graphical objects. Publisher allows you to work with images individually or as part of a collective group.

Selecting multiple items

You can select items individually or simultaneously select a group of items.

To select all the items on a page:

1.   Select *Edit*.

2.   Click *Select All* or press *Ctrl+A*.

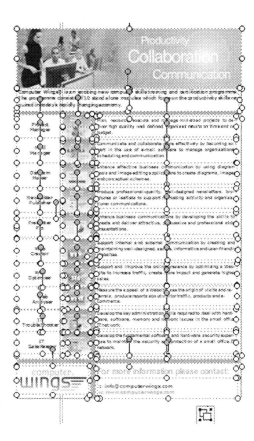

All the items on the open page are selected:

Selecting multiple items

You can select additional items when working with various objects.

To select an additional item:

1. Select an item.

2. Hold the *Shift* key and click on one or more additional items. All the items are selected and you can move or copy the group of items.

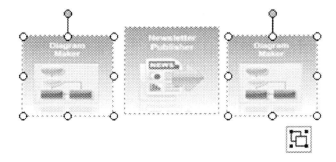

Group

Group

You can group a set of objects into a single object. Any actions are then performed on the single set of objects.

To group multiple objects:

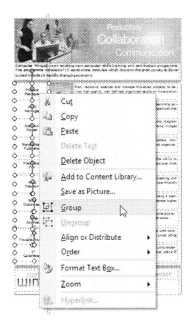

1.   Select the objects you want to group.

2.   Select *Group* from the:

   •   *Arrange* menu.

   •   *Object* menu displayed when you right-click on the group of objects.

You can now work with the group as if it is a single object. For example, you can rotate or flip all the objects in the group simultaneously.

Ungroup

You can ungroup a set of objects by clicking *Ungroup* from the *Arrange* menu, or use the shortcut *Ctrl+Shift+G*.

You can select a single item that is assigned to group by holding the *Shift* key while selecting the individual item. You can work with the individual item without ungrouping the set of objects.

Promote, demote

You can set the order in which objects are displayed. This can be used to overlay pictures over each other.

The following example explains how you overlay a picture over another picture.

1. Select the picture.

2. Right-click to open the *Object* menu.

3. Select *Bring to Front*.

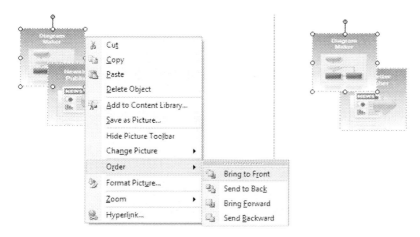

You can also access the *Order* options from the:

- *Standard* toolbar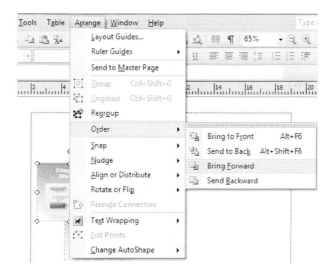

- *Arrange* menu

Colour

Colour adds considerably to the visual range and appeal of your publication.

Background colour

You can apply a background colour to your publication as follows:

1. Open your publication.

2. Select *Background* from the *Format* menu or select it from the *Publisher Tasks* menu.

    The *Background* options are displayed.

3. Select a colour and click on the arrow to indicate whether you want to apply your changes to only the current page or to all pages in the publication.

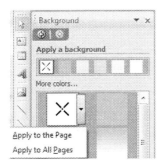

By selecting *More colours* you can access additional colour palettes.

Changing the colour in a picture

You can change the colour of a picture as follows:

1. Select the picture.

2. Select *Picture* from the *Format* menu, or select *Format Picture* from the *Object* menu for the picture.

3. Open the *Picture* tab and select *Recolor*.

4. Select the colour you want to apply to the picture. A preview of the picture with the selected colour is displayed. You can test other colours before selecting *Apply* to apply your changes to the picture.

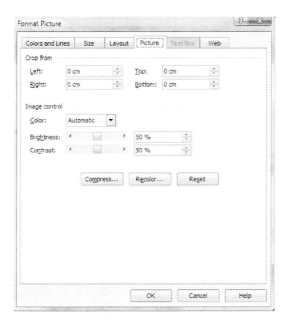

Applying border colours

You can change the colours applied to borders.

To change the colour applied to a text box border:

1.   Select the text box.

2.   Open the *Format Text Box* dialogue by either selecting *Format Text Box* from the *Format* menu, or from the *Object* menu displayed when you right-click on the text box.

3.   Open the *Colour and Lines* tab.

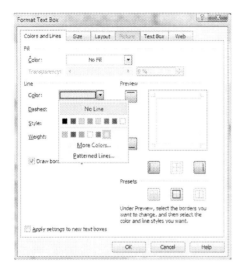

4.   Select the colour you want to apply to the text box borders. The colour selected is displayed in the *Preview* area.

5.   Select *OK* to apply your border colours to the text box.

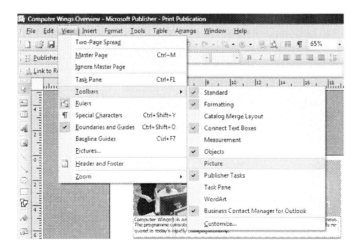

To activate the toolbar for working with pictures, select *Toolbars* from the *View* menu and click on *Picture*.

Click *Picture* to activate the toolbar. The *Picture* toolbar is displayed:

The *Picture* toolbar is a floating toolbar, this means it floats over your working documents and you can adjust the formatting of your picture as you require.

Quick Quiz

Select the correct answer from the following multiple-choice questions:

1   Which one of the following is a free, open-source image file format?

    a   TIFF

    b   JPEG

    c   PNG

    d   BMP

2   Which word completes this sentence?

    _____ objects allows you to move, rotate, and resize a number of objects as a single unit.

    a   Combining

    b   Grouping

    c   Merging

    d   Amalgamating

3   Where can you find options to position a picture precisely?

    a   *Format > Picture > Position tab*

    b   *Arrange > Picture > Position tab*

    c   *Format > Picture > Layout tab*

    d   *Arrange > Picture > Layout tab*

4   Which tool would you use to reduce a picture by removing parts of it?

    a   Chop tool

    b   Crop tool

    c   Reduce tool

    d   Delete tool

Answers to Quick Quiz

1   c   PNG

2   b   Grouping

3   c   *Format* > *Picture* > *Layout tab*

4   b   Crop tool

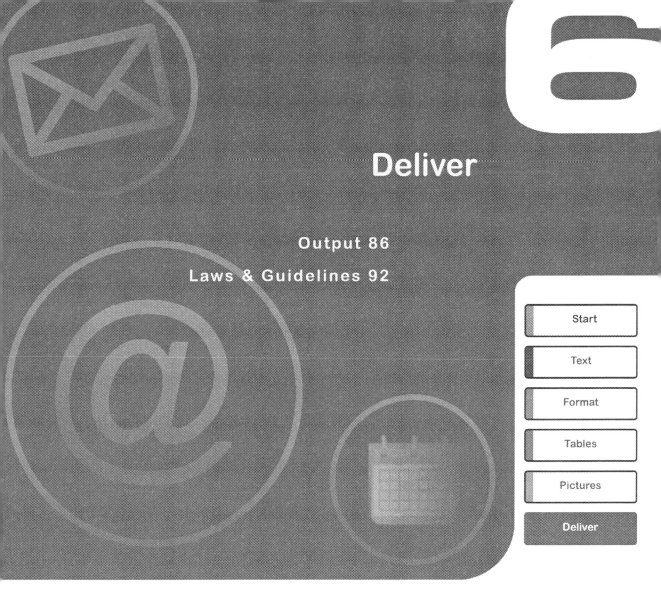

Deliver

Output 86
Laws & Guidelines 92

Start

Text

Format

Tables

Pictures

Deliver

Measuring points

- Preview a newsletter project including spell-checking and proof-reading, and make changes where necessary
- Choose basic print options, and print
- Output files in PDF format
- Publish a newsletter on a website
- Publish a newsletter within an email
- Be aware of data protection legislation or conventions in your country

- Be aware of copyright laws and their impact for downloading content from the Internet, and in terms of image usage, and apportion due credit for use
- Recognise the significance of disability / equality legislation in helping to provide all users with access to information
- Recognise organisation layout guidelines or branding specifications

Introduction

Editing and proofing text are important tasks to carry out when finalising any publication. This is to ensure that the quality of the information you create is maintained in both terms of look and actual content.

This chapter explains how you can preview, print or output your publications for different communication channels, and explains how you use Publisher for creating a website. This chapter also deals with some of the legislation that is relevant to external publications and also highlights the use of internal branding specifications.

Output

It is good practice to always preview and spell check a copy of your publication prior to printing. Publisher makes it easy to share, print and publish your marketing material or other information by converting your publication to view by email, pdf or on the Web.

Previewing

Print Preview

To proof a publication, select *Print Preview* from the *File* menu, or in the *Print* dialogue before you print a document. You can review the *pagination* and layout of your information using *Print Preview*.

Spell checking

You should always perform a spell check before you finalise a document. To spell check a completed publication, select *Spelling* from the *Tools* menu or press *F7*.

Printing

To print your publication:

1.   Select *Print* from the *File* menu to open the print dialogue. Open the *Publication and Paper Settings* tab.

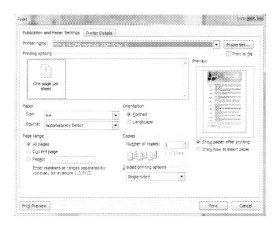

2.   Check that the printer name is correct. If you have access to more than one printer, you can specify the printer you want to use for the publication from the list available.

3.   Check that the paper orientation is correct.

4.   Specify the pages you want printed and the number of copies you want to print

5.   Use *Print Preview* to review how the document will look when printed or select *Print* to send the document to the printer.

Creating PDFs

You can also use an add-in feature to create a fixed format version of your publication. Fixed file formats create an image file of your document that cannot be easily altered. The integrity of the document can be maintained.

You can apply an add-in feature to Publisher that can be used for creating:

- XML Paper Specification (.xps) files

- Portable Document Format (.pdf) files.

PDF is the more established of the two types and is available across a wide range of Operating Systems. XPS is free and support is included in Windows.

The *Save as PDF* or *XPS add-in* for Microsoft Office 2007 must already be installed before you can save and export files in .pdf or .xps format.

You will also need a viewer for working with XPS files. This viewer is available from www.microsoft.com.

Once you have installed your add-ins, you can create a PDF or XPS file as follows:

1. Select *Publish as PDF or XPS* from the *File* menu.

2. Specify the name for the publication.

3. Select the file type, for example .pdf.

4. Select *Publish*.

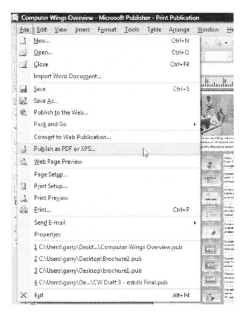

You can specify the print quality you want to apply. If your publication is mainly for online use, then print quality is secondary to file size and you can select *Minimum Size* for your publication. If your document is for printing purposes, you should specify *High Print Quality* to ensure print quality.

Publishing with email

Email is a powerful way to disseminate your marketing materials quickly and efficiently. Modern email packages allow you to embed your content into the body of the email message or include as a pdf attachment.

You can create an email from a Publisher publication as follows:

Embedding

1. Select and copy the content you wish to include in an email.

    *   It is good practice to group all images and content in your publication before you copy.

2. Switch from Publisher to your email package.

3. *Paste* into the body text section of the email message.

4. Check your content has displayed as you wish:

    • You will also need to check and switch on the HTML or Rich Text message format in your email package, so that the images or graphical options are displayed.

5. Click *Send*.

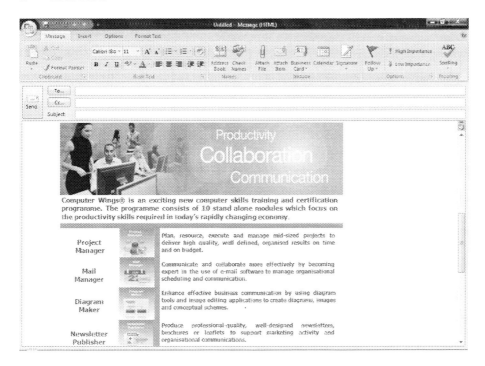

Attaching

1. Open the publication.

2. Select *Send E-mail* from the *File* menu.

3. Click on *Send Publication as Attachment*. A blank email is opened containing the publication as an attachment.

4. Complete your email and send.

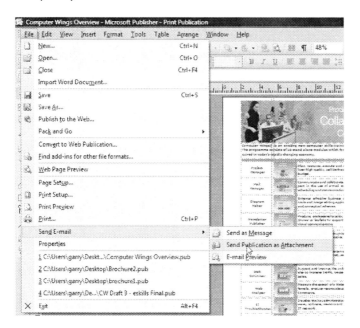

Publishing on a website

Creating a website

You can use *Publisher* for creating websites.

To create a website with Publisher:

1. Select *New* from the *File* menu.

2. Click on *Web Sites* in the *Publication Types* dialogue.

3. Select the design you want to apply from the selection available.

4. Double-click or click *Create*. The *Easy Web Site Builder* dialogue is displayed:

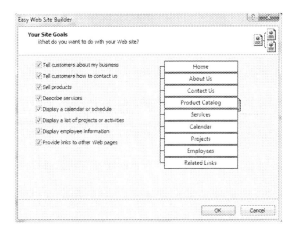

5. Specify the purpose of your website by clicking on the various options available. These options are used for establishing the layout of your website. Select *OK* when you have completed your selection.

    A new publication project is created based on your selections.

6. Select *OK*.

You can now create content for your website in the various pages.

If you want to create a website that does not contain any pre-defined formatting, select *Blank Sizes* when selecting the website type and select the size you want to use.

Previewing website

You can preview your website by selecting *Web Page Preview* from the *File* menu. An *Explorer* window is opened containing a preview of your website.

You can use this preview to check whether your website is working correctly. You can switch/'toggle' between the various web pages to view content and to ensure that information is working correctly. You can also check any links and hyperlinks and ensure that they resolve to the correct address or link.

You can also check the colour scheme applied to your website and change any aspects that you want to improve.

Publishing your website

To publish a website, you need to have a subscription to a web hosting service. This service is provided by an Internet Service Provider (ISP) and includes the provision of:

*   Web storage space.

*   A Uniform Resource Locator (URL) which is the address through which your website can be accessed by other people using a web protocol such as HTTP.

When you are ready to publish your website, contact your ISP to obtain details for the URL of your website and the storage location.

To publish your website:

1. Select *Publish to the Web* from the *File* menu. The *Publish to the Web* dialogue is displayed.

2. Specify the URL of the web server you will be using in the *File Name* field.

3. Select *Save*. If requested, specify your user name and password and click *OK* to continue.

    The directory that is linked with the URL you specified is displayed in the *Publish to Web* dialogue.

4. Click twice on the folder you want to use for storing your website.

5. Select *Index* as the default name for your home page. This prevents other people from viewing the list of files you used for creating your website.

6. Select *Save*.

7. Click *OK* when prompted to complete.

Your website is published to the specified location and can be accessed using the assigned URL.

Laws and Guidelines

Data protection legislation

National data protection legislation defines the legal basis for the handling of personal information in a particular country and provides the basis by which individuals can govern the control of information about themselves. Such legislation typically confers rights on individuals who have their personal information stored as well as obligations on those who store such data.

The principles of data protection require that personal data should be processed fairly and lawfully. In order for data to be classed as fairly processed, at least one of the following six conditions must be applicable to the data:

- The data subject (the person whose data is stored) has consented to the processing.

- Processing is necessary for the performance of a contract (any processing not directly required to complete a contract would not be fair).

- Processing is required under a legal obligation (other than one stated in the contract).

- Processing is necessary to protect the vital interests of the data subject's rights.

- Processing is necessary to carry out any public functions.

- Processing is necessary in order to pursue the legitimate interests of the data controller or third parties (unless it could unjustifiably prejudice the interests of the data subject).

You should be aware of the applicable legislation in your own country.

Copyright and the Internet

Copyright material published on the Internet will generally be protected in the same way as material in other media. Copyright is protected internationally through international treaties, such as, the Berne Convention to which over 160 countries are parties to. Before the Berne Convention, national copyright laws usually only applied for works created within each country.

Copyright has two main purposes, namely the protection of the author's right to obtain commercial benefit from valuable work and the protection of the author's general right to control how a work is used. Almost all works are copyrighted the moment they are written and no copyright notice is required.

You should be aware that if publishing material from other sources the express permission of the copyright owner (unless copyright exceptions apply) is required. In all cases, copies should be acknowledged as far as is practicable. In addition, many websites will include a copyright statement setting out exactly the way in which materials on the site may be used.

You should also be aware that many online resources may have been published illegally without the permission of the copyright owners. Any subsequent use of the materials, such as printing, or copying and pasting, may also be illegal.

For further details on copyright requirements within your own country please refer to your own applicable national legislation.

Disability / equality legislation

Disability legislation prohibits direct discrimination, victimisation and harassment and promotes equality for disabled people. Disability legislation, in particular, makes it unlawful to discriminate against people in respect of their disabilities in relation to such matters as employment, the provision of goods and services, education and transport.

At national level, policies relating to people with disabilities reflect the diversity of cultures and legislative frameworks in the EU Member States. The definitions and the criteria for determining disability are currently laid down in national legislation and administrative practices and differ across the current Member States according to their perceptions of, and approaches to, disability.

You should be aware of your own applicable national legislation as well as relevant international directives.

Organisational branding specifications

You should be aware that organisations frequently apply an in-house style guide to be applied to all in-house communications produced. Such style guides are designed to ensure that staff collaborate to present a consistent and professional corporate image in all communications. Style guides would typically provide guidance on use of corporate logos, emails, letters, faxes, newsletters and other publications.

Quick Quiz

Select the correct answer from the following multiple-choice questions.

1   What is the purpose of outputting files in a PDF format?

   a   To apply an alternative editable word processing format

   b   To virus protect a document before publication

   c   To have a high quality, professional-looking print or output

   d   To prepare a document version control on a QMS server

2   Choose from one of the following to complete the sentence.

   Data Protection legislation provides for the _____ of Data Holders.

   a   Rights

   b   Liabilities

   c   Obligations

   d   Needs

3   You wish to spell check your work before publishing. Which keyboard shortcuts will you use?

   a   F1

   b   F7

   c   F3

   d   F4

4   You wish to include your publication as part of an eshot. Which message format will ensure it displays correctly?

   a   Plain Text Format

   b   Rich Text Format

   c   Simple Text Format

   d   Proprietary Text Format

Answers to Quick Quiz

1   c   To have a high quality, professional looking print or output

2   c   Obligations

3   b   F7

4   b   Rich Text Format